*For Lloyd Smith, who loves plants
(especially the ones that eat animals), and
for all botanists who cherish the GREEN! —ND*

For Lucy, Sophie, and Emily —ES

GREEN

The Story of Plant Life
on Our Planet

NICOLA DAVIES

illustrated by
EMILY SUTTON

CANDLEWICK PRESS

This tree doesn't look like it's doing very much.

It doesn't move or even make a sound unless the wind blows—

it just stands there in the sunlight, **big** and GREEN.

But in fact, this tree is busy:
beneath the bark, water rushes in
from the roots, traveling up the trunk
and through every branch and twig
to reach the leaves.

An invisible gas called carbon dioxide
is making its way into the leaves, too.
It is part of the air that swooshes in
through tiny holes—too tiny to see—
all over each leaf.

What's more, every leaf is busy
soaking up sunlight.

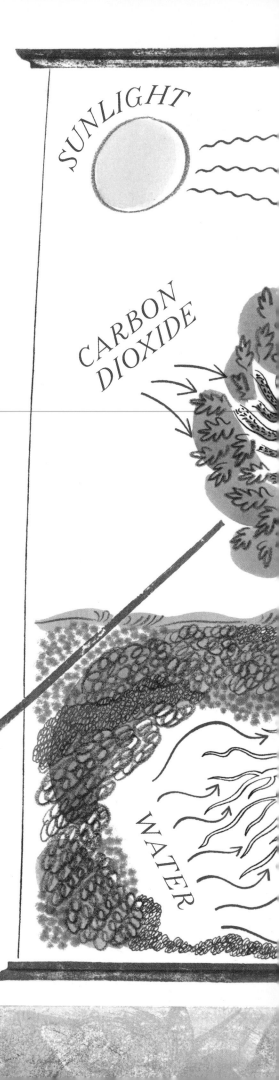

SUNLIGHT

CARBON DIOXIDE

WATER

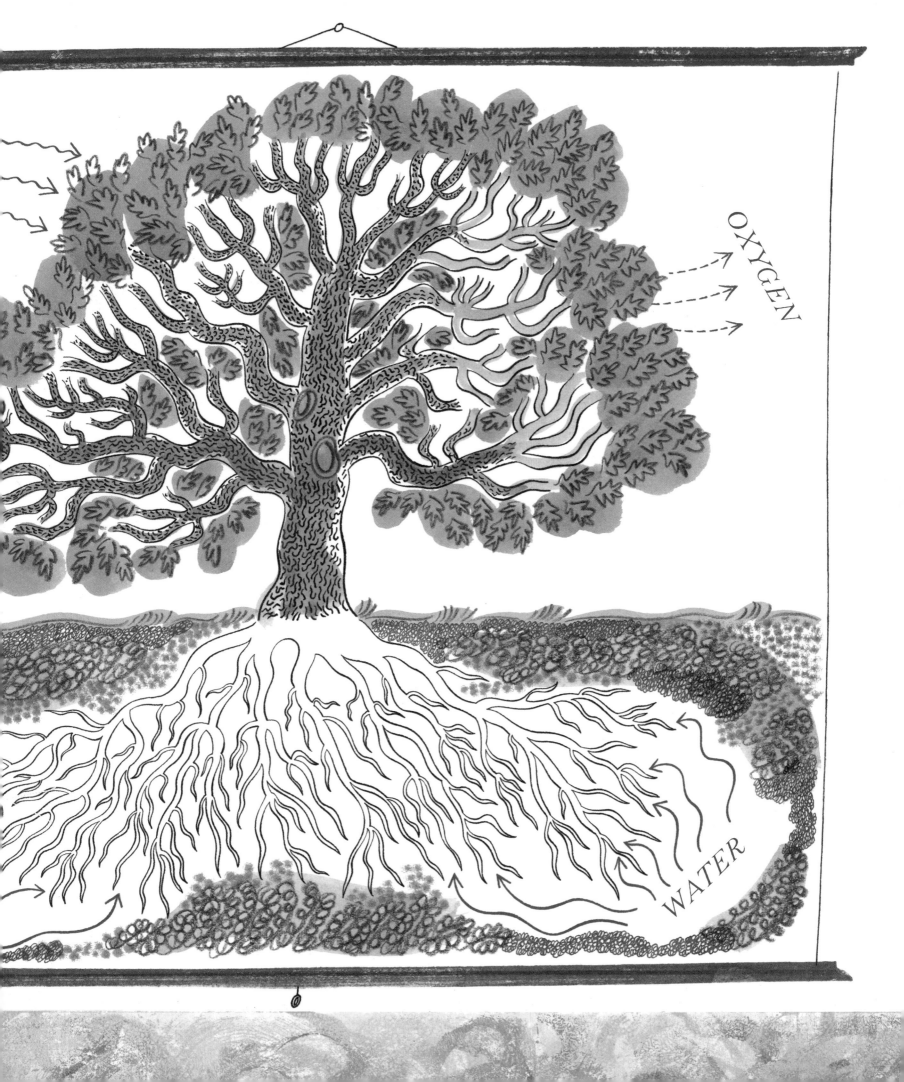

OXYGEN

WATER

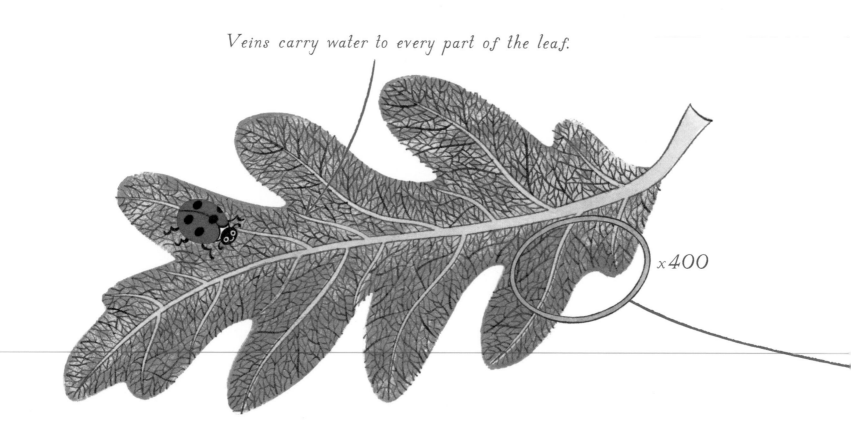

Veins carry water to every part of the leaf.

x400

Leaves may look as thin as paper, but under a microscope you can see that they are made of layers of tiny, tiny parts called cells. Each cell is packed tight with bundles of the greenest green called chloroplasts.

These chloroplasts are the busiest part of the tree. Their green isn't just a color . . . *this* green catches the energy in sunlight and uses it to turn carbon dioxide and water into sugar and another gas called oxygen.

The tree uses the sugar as food to make more leaves and roots and branches, and breathes the oxygen out through the holes in its leaves.

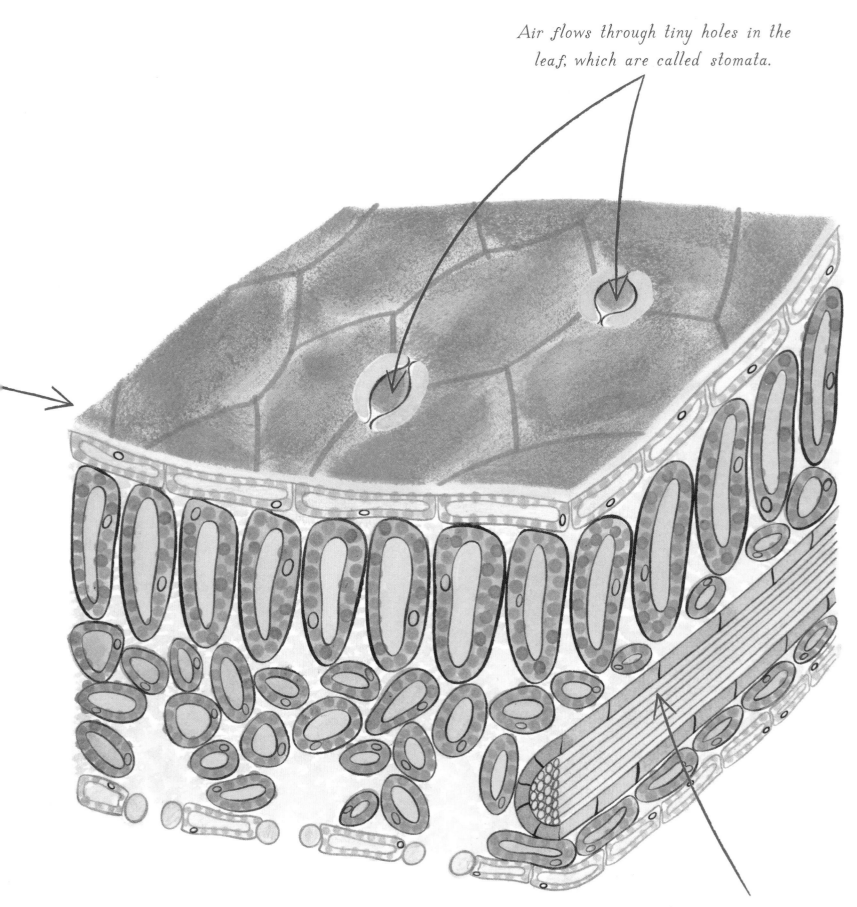

Air flows through tiny holes in the leaf, which are called stomata.

Veins are made of bundles of tiny tubes that bring water up from the roots.

The name for this process is photosynthesis.

All plants do it. It's the reason why they are green . . .
and green plants are everywhere.

Living things depend on plants for the food they make
and the oxygen that they breathe out.

*The arrows in this picture point to what each creature eats. If you follow them,
you will see that even meat-eating animals depend on plants for their food.*

Living things breathe in oxygen and use it to get energy from their food in a process called **respiration**.

This process is the opposite of photosynthesis. Together, the two keep our air in balance . . . just right for life.

Respiration USES oxygen and MAKES carbon dioxide.

Photosynthesis *USES* carbon dioxide and *MAKES* oxygen.

But it wasn't always like this. Four billion years ago, before plants existed, Earth's air was toxic. Only the tiniest of creatures, called microbes, could survive.

First simple microbes

The ancestors of plants were very simple. They could stick together in chains and blobs.

Then, some new microbes came along. They were tiny—just one cell big—but they formed blobby mats in the warm, shallow seas, and their photosynthesis put oxygen into the air for the first time.

2.7 BILLION YEARS AGO

Microbes begin to put oxygen into the air.

This oxygen made more life possible.
Bigger plants and animals in the sea . . .

1 BILLION YEARS AGO   *550 MILLION YEARS AGO (MYA)*   *530 MYA*

First seaweeds   *Many seaweeds and invertebrates*   *First fish*   *First plants on land*

and then on land.

MYA · 419 MYA · 385 MYA

First insects on land　*Many new kinds of big fish*　*First land vertebrates and first forests*

During the Carboniferous Period, there were forests where trees reached 100 feet (30 meters) in height.

After a long time, huge swampy forests grew and covered the planet.

When trees and plants in the forests died, they sank into muddy swamps— trapping the carbon dioxide that was stored inside their leaves, roots, and branches underground.

These forests were filled with life, from huge amphibians to giant insects, as well as the first reptiles.

For 60 million years, those forests flourished, and whenever plants died, they fell into the swamp . . .

were buried in mud . . .

and were crushed under rocks.

Long after the ancient swamp forests had died out and vanished, their remains lay under the earth. Over many millions of years, those remains turned into coal, oil, and gas— which we know today as fossil fuels.

Locked inside these fossil fuels was a huge store of carbon dioxide, as well as energy from sunlight. Human beings used this energy to create our modern world, burning coal, oil, and gas to heat houses, power factories, and fuel cars and planes.

In just 200 years, we have released most of the carbon dioxide that those ancient forests locked up over the course of 60 million years.

The band of air around the Earth is called the atmosphere. It's made up of layers of gases, about 60 miles (100 kilometers) deep.

Carbon dioxide is like a blanket around the Earth that prevents heat from escaping. Every bit of carbon dioxide we add to the air makes the blanket even warmer, messing up the weather and causing droughts, floods, and storms. It's why our planet is getting hotter, and why the climate is changing.

From space, it looks like

a haze of blue, wrapped around the whole planet.

But plants can help by making shade
to keep the hot ground cool . . .

and breathing water into
the air to create rain.

Most of all, plants help to restore the balance
of the air: they trap energy from sunlight with
their greenness and lock up carbon dioxide
in their leaves and roots and branches.

Plants don't do all this alone. They work together with other living things, such as animals, which pollinate their flowers and spread their seeds, and fungi, which wrap around their roots and help them to reach for goodness in the soil.

Plants also work with one another. All around the world, there are communities of plants: great green nations.

Taiga forests, also called boreal forests, cover more than one tenth of the Earth's surface.

Forests of many kinds grow wherever there is enough rain for trees to flourish—from the taiga that covers the land around the cold northern regions of our planet . . .

to the tropical forests that once made a green belt around the Earth's equator. All of these forests take carbon dioxide from the air and lock it up in their trunks and branches.

Tropical forests need protection: they are being cut down for wood and to make space to grow crops such as palm oil.

Where it's too dry for trees to grow, there are grasslands and prairies, with deep, rich soils that can also store carbon dioxide.

Many grasslands have been used for farming, but if too many crops are grown, or too many animals grazed, the soils become bare and can be swept away by the wind or rain.

Even the open ocean is green,
with billions of microscopic plants called
phytoplankton floating near the sunlit surface.
These tiny plants make more than half of the
oxygen in the air we breathe!

Every day, 8 million new bits of plastic find their way into the world's oceans, making
it harder for marine life to survive—especially as climate change continues to warm the water.

There are also seaweed jungles, close to the shore, and seagrass beds, which live in shallow water. They soak up carbon dioxide even faster than forests on land do.

All of these green nations are under threat. On land, humans have cut many forests down to make way for farms, roads, and cities—and we have polluted the oceans with plastic.

This means they need our help and protection.
They need us to remember that GREEN
is the most important color in the world.